The Wind Blows and The Flowers Dance is a REAL love story. It is not just a story of deep love between two people. It is how love even in the face of death's tragedy never leaves you and will show up because it lives in your heart. Terre's beautiful art and words offer the raw truth about death and about her courage to continue when it seemed most impossible. If you find yourself looking for a book about grief, this book will offer you REAL hope because it is about REAL love.

~ Beth Kean
Retired Bereavement Coordinator Hospice

What a treat! This beautiful book opens a window to one person's experience of the mystery and pain of death, then gently ushers us to an awakening of new life. Drawing on a deep well of insights and emotions, and using a minimum of words to express them, we become a special guest invited to witness what it means to be human in all its grand, devastating, and life-giving moments. A joy to read.

~ Dr. Harry Eberts
Pastor, First Presbyterian Church of Santa Fe, New Mexico

This book will be hard to put down. It is healing medicine that penetrates to the deepest part of one's nature. Her artistic ability shines a soft and embracing light into the process of grief. Terre awakens all the sense doors and turns the grieving process into a welcoming experience.

~ Ralph Steele
Author, *Tending the Fire*
Guiding Teacher of Life Transition Meditation Center

With poignancy and humor, Ms. Reed provides an insightful journey through the process of grief following the loss of a spouse or partner. The author expertly captures the gamut of emotions leading up to and following death. I cried, laughed and revisited my own grief. I came away with a better understanding and a greater sense of closure around my own personal loss. An accomplished artist, five of her paintings accentuate the narrative.

~ Leland D. Shaeffer
Widower, Los Angeles

I feel blessed to travel this journey with you, so creatively expressed, as well as thoroughly and deeply experienced. You show us how learning and experiencing the power of the present moment can serve as an anchor to touch the losses and wounds of the past and a tool to move forward, one step at a time to renewal, over and over again. Those who experience grief will find support and sustenance to carry on in your book.

~ Bette Betts
Licensed Clinical Social Worker

Having lost to death my partner of forty-seven years, many of your words expressing the immense pain and emptiness resonates in my life. Your ability to put into words the feeling of aloneness with the desire to hide from the outside world described my innermost feelings upon my wife's death—I was instantly a widower. A very insightful work.

~ Tony Alarid
Widower, Santa Fe, New Mexico

Terre has compiled a tough, tender and touching journey from the loss of her beloved husband to the nourishment and intensity of self-discovery. From opening to close, this memoir accompanied by five gorgeous paintings and nine philosophically precise poems of warmth and love is a treasure, a polished and radiant work!

~ Kathleen Gilbert
Poet, Four-time winner of the
Browning Society Gita Specker Award

Beautiful . . . painful . . .important. A process for each widow to find the path to peace and joy. While you may never "get over it," you probably don't want to. The prize of Terre's journey is learning to live beautifully with it. Her book is a "must read" for the widow to be, the widow of reality, and the widow of rebirth.

~ Dona Cook
Widow, Santa Fe, New Mexico

THE WIND BLOWS AND
THE FLOWERS DANCE

THE WIND BLOWS AND THE FLOWERS DANCE

AN ARTIST SHARES HER LIFE FROM LOSS TO RENEWAL

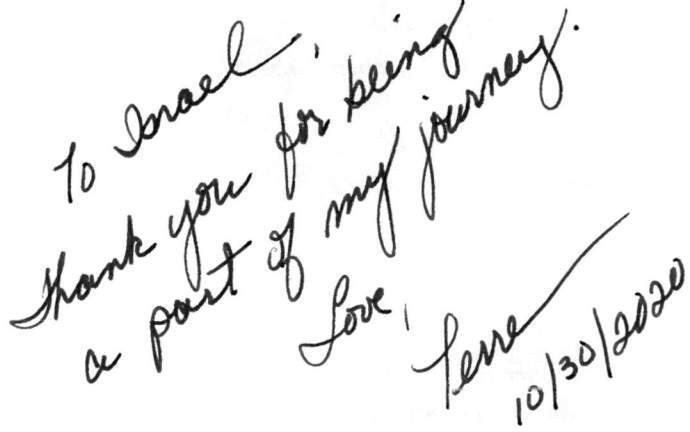

TERRE REED

For

Liam, Brian, and Claudia

The Wind Blows and the Flowers Dance
Terre Reed
October, 2019
30" X 36"
Oil on Canvas

To view this painting in color, go to
TerreReed.com

Contents

Part One

Loss

Part Two
Transition

Part Three
Renewal

Part Four

The Poems

Preface

"Real grieving refuses to remain Life goes on, no matter what. Within five months, I lost my husband and my forty-year marriage. I was also the first among my group of friends to lose a spouse, to no longer be a couple. The loss, the process of coping with my new self and then reshaping life is the theme of this book. I share my story with you as my form of companionship, compassion, and empathy for your experience.

My reading brought me to the Bardo, that part of Buddhism which expresses a theory of the period of time after death and before rebirth. Although I was still alive, I suffered a loss so great and so traumatic that I realized I, too, experienced a death, my own living death. I had to accept and rediscover myself. I had to create a new life for myself. Hence, a Living Bardo.

From this inspiration, the book came together quite naturally in these three parts: Loss, Transition, and Renewal. The Poems, Part Four, express raw, real emotions during this healing process.

Creativity is significant. I express emotions and thoughts in prose, in poetry or through paintings. And I share all of this because I have come to a basic truth—sharing is a true path after the loss of a loved one.

I include a schematic titled, "Vocabulary of the Living Bardo." As I was sorting out my feelings, I realized vocabulary around grief evolves into its own timeline. Perhaps you will identify with where you are on your journey.

Voluntarily and involuntarily, we move through grief. It is my hope that this book will give you a small measure of comfort and direction. You are not alone. Your feelings are valid. It is possible to be happy again.

Part One
Loss

Charlie's Red Wings
Terre Reed
May, 2019
30"x 36"
Oil on Canvas

To view this painting in color, go to
TerreReed.com

2

1

It's a Mystery

"Real grieving refuses to remain in sorrow."
The Smell of Rain on Dust by Martin Prechtel

Liam was eight when we realized Charlie's passing was near. He and his mother arrived late at night. As soon as the car had barely stopped in the driveway, Liam hopped out. "Where's Charlie?"

"He's in the house sleeping," I answered. "But I'm sure he would like to see you. Let's go find him."

"Hi Charlie," Liam said softly as he approached the bed.

Charlie opened his eyes. Smiling, he reached out a hand. "Hi Liam. It's good to see you."

Liam was signed up for Adventure Camp, a high-energy day camp for boys and girls. Going to Charlie's bedside every day, Liam would say, "Good morning, Charlie," and tell him what he was doing that day—swimming, rock climbing, kayaking, bowling. "See you later," was his good-bye. Even when Charlie could no longer speak, or open his eyes, Liam would go to him, talk to him, tell him about his day.

Charlie passed on Friday afternoon while Liam was at camp. When his mother picked him up, she told him he had died. Charlie's body was still at the house. Did he want to see Charlie one last time? "Yes," was his answer.

The entry door from the garage to the house creaked when opened and slammed loudly when left to close on its own, announcing his arrival. Liam stomped up the stairs and marched to Charlie's bedside. Stopping for only a moment, he turned and walked out.

For three days after the memorial service, he lived in a 'tent' that he built in the living room with sheets and blankets over tables and chairs. He made a cardboard keypad. You had to ask for the code before you could enter.

* * *

"You know Granny," Liam says a few months later, "I've been thinking. I'm not sure I believe in heaven and hell. I mean, I think telling someone they have to go to hell forever is rather harsh."

"What about the really bad people? Murderers for instance," I ask.

"Well, okay. They can go. I also don't believe in angels with wings and feathers."

"I agree with that. Charlie would look pretty funny wearing feathers and wings, wouldn't he!" From now on I'm going to look at angels in Renaissance paintings with comic relief.

He continues, "Maybe when your soul leaves your body, somewhere a baby is born and you jump into it."

"That's a possibility. There are people who believe that theory. There is even a name for it. It's called reincarnation. The truth is that we really don't know what happens to our spirit when we die because none of us have ever done it. It's a mystery."

"Well, that really sucks if that's what happens!"

"Why?"

"Because then you have to go to school all over again."

2

The News

"There are powers who are not the
prerogatives of kings."
Antigone by Sophocles

Seemingly, out of nowhere comes the kidney cancer diagnosis with the kidney surgeon's opinion that this is not an emergency. We try to relax with the positive news.

Worry because we don't know what's going on; relief upon seeing Charlie's primary care doctor quickly and making a plan. More worry when we learn there IS something big.

Five days elapse from serious pain, diagnosis, and surgery being scheduled. It's hard to think in this holding pattern of stress—our lives move in slow motion trying to process the magnitude of it all. It takes every bit of energy to focus on today. We are in shock.

3

The First Thing Is . . .

"The law of Zeus - we suffer into wisdom."
Antigone by Sophocles

Shock ripples through our family and friends—phones ringing with concern, fears, questions, and recommendations. What do you really know about this doctor? You must get a second opinion. University of New Mexico has a great cancer center. Where are you going to go to have the surgery? I would go to MD Anderson in Houston. And, why did this happen?

Charlie's pain is compounded by anxiety. He can't deal with reading research papers or making phone calls and asking questions. I do that. And, I am not a linear thinker. My thoughts jump all around; frequently I think out loud.

"The first thing is," says Charles, "I want to heal where I am most comfortable, and that would be at home. After surgery, I want to come home."

4

Meeting Charles

My Memory

It rains in February in San Francisco. A lot. If I can survive all the rainy days in this month, then the rest of the year will be easy. Today is Saturday and hallelujah, surprise! The sun is shining. The air smells fresh and clean. All I want is to go outside, sit in that expansive feeling of warmth, and maybe read a book.

Rarely do I have time to be in the small private back yard. It really isn't landscaped, just small green weeds instead of grass with bare spots enclosed by a wooden fence. But today it is sunny and inviting. I have no outdoor furniture, but I see a small, old weathered bench sitting next to the building. That will do. I sit down for one moment, then jump up. It is unsafe. It could collapse, sideways. I can fix this. I just need a nail.

What is that racket? It's Saturday. What's going on over there? Even though the fence is maybe six feet or more tall, the elevations between my property and the one next door are such that my outdoor space is much lower than their patio. I can see worker bees from the waist up focused on building something. Ah, they have nails.

"Excuse me. Excuse me," I say, standing near the fence, trying to get someone's attention. A burly guy with wild curly hair and a beard, wearing railroad overalls with no shirt, turns and smiles. "Could I borrow a nail?" I ask.

"What do you want with a nail?" he replies.

"Well, I have this wobbly bench," I say, pointing. "And I'm sure I could fix it if I had a nail. I notice you are building something, so you must have nails and maybe I could have one?"

"Let me see that." He says. I pass it over. He and the bench disappear. When he comes back, he hands a very sturdy bench to me. "Would you like to come over and see my project?" he invites.

"Not now," is my reply. "I am just going to sit and enjoy the sun. But I appreciate your help. Thank you."

It feels good to sit on the bench and lean back against the warmth of the building. I close my eyes. Moments later I hear scraping, like something being dragged over flagstone. I look as he pulls up a chair and sets it at an angle facing me. He slouches in the chair, puts his feet on top of the fence, (my fence), closing his eyes as he tilts his head back to the sun.

Clasping his hands across his belly, he looks like he could stay there all afternoon.

"Seems like a good idea," he smiles, as we eye each other.

5

The Way It Began

Another Memory

"Being alive is what it is all about."
"Hero with A Thousand Faces,"
NPR Interview with Joseph Campbell

I walk into the restaurant you are building, curious and wanting to say hello. In contrast to you and your crew, I am wearing a three-piece suit; I look like business. The place smells of sawdust—inside walls still in see-through framing. Late afternoon light coming in the spaces that will be windows.

I look around, orienting myself—each person is busy with his task of measuring, pounding, cutting. There you are, deep in conversation with a man and a woman, who would later be identified as the owners. I just stand there.

One by one the workers notice me, look at you, then back at me. One by one, each stands up, stopping what they are doing, until we are all standing, looking at each other. As the room falls silent, the owners step back from their conversation, staring at me. The energy shift causes you to swivel your head around and see me. You blush with recognition, from the top of your forehead to the part of your chest that is revealed before disappearing into your shirt. And for a moment, it feels like no one is breathing.

Who knew how many dozens of projects there were to come, or how many times I would drop in. Each time, your eyes lit up, happy to see me. But, that moment sealed the connection between us.

I found it refreshing that you didn't have a desk job. I liked that it hadn't occurred to you to comb your curly hair, that your thighs felt like steel, and your body scent was ignited by physical labor at the end of the day.

I liked the way you took time to think things through, unconsciously scratching your red-brown beard under your chin or slowly folding up an old wooden ruler in a moment of contemplation. I liked the way you and your crew would enjoy a beer at the end of the day, sitting in the middle of the project.

"It is good," you'd say, "to take time to appreciate what has been accomplished today."

I liked the way things were.

6

Uncomplicated

"You are not a wave, you're part of the ocean."
Tuesday's with Morrie by Mitch Albom

The surgeon appears to be in his early forties, so he should be on top of his game. He has done maybe five hundred of these surgeries over the past six years, and in his opinion, this one appears to be uncomplicated.

We look at the x-rays together: he points out the mass and compares it to the other kidney. From his experience and looking at the images, he estimates the mass to be about the size of a Rubik's cube. It appears to be contained within the kidney. Because of its size, he plans on taking the whole kidney as well as the adrenal gland.

Bottom line: We agree. This seems to be a straight-forward surgery. Charlie has an immediate rapport with this doctor. The man seems qualified and we see no reason to go anywhere else.

We are consciously shifting from depression, anxiety, and sickness to gratitude and joy. Gratitude this mass is now discovered. Gratitude that there are capable health professionals who are kind, compassionate, and really can address his pain and suffering. We respect and appreciate their desire to remove the kidney and mass under the best possible circumstances.

7

Working with Charlie

My Memory

"Many bad spots in our best times,
many good ones in our worst."
A Grief Observed by C.S. Lewis

"It's just as easy for me to make two or more of something as it is to make one," is Charlie's motto. "By the time I do the drawings and the set up, I might as well make two. We can always use an extra Adirondack chair, or picture frame or cabinet." Or house.

The cost of building two houses that are similar is cheaper than building one, especially in energy and labor. And it's faster. When the framers frame or the concrete trucks pour, they move from one house to the other as if it were all one big project. The hard part is scheduling, but once they arrive, they stay until their job is done.

A house is a three-dimensional puzzle. To us, building is a game. He is thinking how fast can I build this; I am thinking how can I make this the most appealing and saleable? But once the design is agreed upon and the drawings complete, almost no changes are allowed. Stay in budget and stick to the time frame.

The first time we did a lot split and built two houses, we went as far in tandem as we financially could. Then, due to Charlie's reputation, the quality of the home, and our good fortune, one house went under contract. We finished it, sold it, and then finished and sold the second one. The sale of the first house paid for finishing the second, leaving enough money to start the next project without a bank.

"You sold this house too fast, Terre," Charlie said, really annoyed as I proudly presented him with yet another full priced offer. "You sold the last one too fast, too."

"What do you mean? I thought that was my job," is my retort. "Together, we set the price. You are getting exactly what you want. I am bringing you the full price! And now you are complaining?"

"But you sold it out from under me. I haven't even finished this one and it's gone already. And you did that to the last one, too. I need a chance to enjoy them a bit, maybe even keep one.

"Now you tell me this?"

"I didn't realize it until you did it, again."

"It's what I do and I'm good at it. You say go, and *I GO*. I'm not going to apologize for doing my job." I am exasperated.

"It's not about the money, Terre. Building is what I do. This house has a piece of me in it. I don't want to be in such a rush."

Exhaling, I say in a low voice, "Charlie, I accepted the offer. The house is now under contract. We don't have a choice." He nods, looking down.

Silence.

We are both thinking, each in our own corner.

Finally. "This house is turning out really well," I acknowledge. "It's a beauty. And I agree, it is sad to let it go."

More silence.

"What do you think about this?" I ask. "You are going to build another house. That's a given. What do you say the next house, we keep. Until you are ready to do something else, we keep it. What do you say about that?"

"I can live with that, Terre." he says thoughtfully.

Charlie drives the project, choosing the subcontractors, the quality of building materials and commanding the flow of work. I take charge of the visuals, that includes all colors, stains, textures, fixtures, appliances, and landscaping. I have to stay ahead of him as we dance to completion.

Some houses we keep and become rentals; some we sell. Charlie decides. The fun we have working together translates into the final outcome of the project, infusing it with joy and love. We feel it and whoever lives in it feels it, too. "I could live here," we both say upon completion.

Together, we build ten more houses.

8

My Valentine

"Squeeze all the juice from life there is to squeeze."
Breakfast with Buddha by Roland Merullo

It's Saturday. We came home from the hospital yesterday afternoon.

Charlie is roaring back. Yay, for his physical fitness! He has come through surgery with flying colors. "I'm hungry!" He says. Smiling, eager to reconnect with family and friends, the Charlie we know and love is returning. I feel great joy! He will soon be able to be his own advocate. I am ready to reclaim my life!

The sun is shining, the wind is calm, and it is beautiful outside. Thank you, Israel, for building the ramps so I can push Charlie in his wheelchair, and he can be outside in the fresh air. He sits and basks with his eyes closed, resting and soaking up the warmth of the sun's rays. Me, I paint a watercolor of our plum tree. Instead of plums, I paint hearts with "I Love You" on them for my valentine.

9

Blindsided

"... tomorrow is a mystery."
Antigone by Sophocles

We are riding high. We are through it. We have dodged a bullet. Time to celebrate. On the way home from the post-surgery check-up we buy a bottle of cold champagne and a steak to grill, even though it's February.

At 5:15 p.m. the kidney doctor calls, "Can you go to the Emergency Room, right now? I will call them and they will be expecting you."

"But wait. Drop everything and go right now? What is this?"

"His calcium level is dangerously high and can damage the working kidney."

Okay. Turn off the grill, leave the unopened champagne chilling.

Five days later, Charlie is readmitted to the hospital. The latest lab report indicates more cancer. He will have an exhausting day tomorrow while he undergoes test after extensive test, including a complete body bone scan.

Neither of us saw this coming. No one did. Once again, we ask friends and family to hold us in their prayers and thoughts.

10

We Are a Couple

"The eloquence of our affection for one another keeps the
world healthy. Praise and the depth of our grief expressed
for one another keeps the world in love. Love is health."
The Smell of Rain on Dust by Martin Prechtel

Did you ever have a disagreement or an argument with a really
sick person? It's frustrating. I have, but then felt really, really
guilty, as if I'd hit him when he was down.

We talk about the future and I disagree or reject his plans
that are meant to reassure me. We have always been very
independent of each other and all that is changed. In fact,
nothing is the same. Nothing.

I can't love Charles back to wellness. I feel powerless as
he slowly, but steadily deteriorates. I'm afraid of the outcome.
The only thing I can think to do is to love.

An element of grief is creeping into our daily life. This
grief plus disappointment and unfulfilled expectations add up
to depression. I just want to go gangbusters and fight this

cancer. But it is not my call. We have to go at the rate Charlie and his body find comfortable. This frightens me because I don't want to wait, go slow, and be reasonable!

We have a Nepalese singing bowl Charlie bought for an anniversary present. It is a brass bowl with a wooden mallet that makes the most beautiful sound. Instead of yelling my name when he needs help, he chimes the bowl. It is playing its song a lot more now than it ever did. Somehow it takes the edge off of "drop everything and come quickly." The singing bowl transforms our fear and his suffering into a love song.

We are thankful for another day.

11

Playing with Charlie

My Memory

"The most precious gift that marriage gave me was
this constant impact of something very close and intimate
yet all the time unmistakably other,
resistant - in a word, real."
A Grief Observed by C.S. Lewis

"What's your favorite color, Charles?" I ask.

"White. I like white. Before you came along, I didn't know windows or walls could be any other color but white."

"Ah, your eyes have been opened!" I say, enjoying the look on his face.

It is easy to see I like color. I wear it, I paint it, I grow it. Charles, in contrast, has a neutral uniform. Every day he wears a white polo shirt and khaki shorts, almost year-round. When we go out to dinner I ask, "Can you kick it up a notch?"

"What do you mean?" he replies, "I just showered and changed. They're clean."

He likes white. But Charles is not a painter. Therefore, very early on when purple swirls appear on the wall around our clawfoot bathtub in the kitchen, he has to concede: He who holds the paint brush gets to choose the color.

* * *

While he is gone on a three week cycling trip in Europe, I decide, as a surprise, to have his truck repainted. His champion, old, charcoal-gray truck will have new life. Arriving home three days early, the truck is not ready and painting it is no longer a surprise; it's a nice gesture. "It won't be ready for two days," I say, "So, we'll use my car in the meanwhile."

The first thing both of us want when returning to Santa Fe after a trip, is a New Mexico green chile fix for lunch. On our way, with Charlie driving, he stops for a red light. As cross traffic rolls by I spot a bright fuchsia colored truck. Charlie would call that a girly truck.

"See that?" I ask, pointing. "I thought that would be a good color for your truck."

"What? It's not gray?" he reacts, his face starting to register horror.

"Why would I paint it gray? It already was gray. We did that color. I thought it would be good to try something different. Fuchsia is one of the hot new colors today."

"You didn't."

I shrug, "I hold the paint brush."

Smoldering and silent, he immediately changes directions. "Where are you going?" I ask in genuine disbelief. He refuses to answer or look at me. He heads straight for the body shop. Are you kidding me? I think he must be jet-lagged. At the body shop he jumps out, slamming the door, looking for his truck. There it is, in all of its fresh charcoal-gray glory.

I can't resist, "Gotcha."

12

Our New Reality

"Things become very clear when there is no escape."
Comfortable with Uncertainty by Pema Chodron

The diagnosis is stage four renal carcinoma, or kidney cancer that has metastasized or spread to his bones: a cancer lesion on a femur, several sites on a couple of ribs, his right scapula, and the most threatening, lesions on a number of vertebrae along his spine. In other words, his body is riddled with cancer.

After all the doctors leave, I sit near Charlie, on his bed, holding hands, not speaking. How do we take this in? How do we share this news with family? And friends? What do we say to each other?

We are touching that most hidden tender spot where life pivots and reframes. That oh-so-tender spot where there is an inner awareness we dare not name, speak, or admit, because the knowing is the raw realization: *We are looking at death.*

13

What Is Real?

"I walked through an emotional doorway to find joy, rage, and
sorrow woven into a timeless song
of praise and longing."
Judy Tuwaletstiwa, Retrospective Exhibition
Santa Fe, New Mexico

What I know is when someone you love has cancer, you don't
really know what or where is bottom. You don't know what is
a level or even keel. Anchors are a concept, not a reality.

I keep busy, telling myself I am being helpful, doing what
I can. I'm scared. Somehow unloading the dishwasher helps. I
know how important it is to be the advocate for someone who
is suffering. The truth is that I am powerless to heal this man.
On good days, it is easy to pretend that things are almost
normal and I am so hopeful.

I rub his shoulders; I scratch his head. I massage his
feet; he drifts off. I hold his hand while he sleeps because I
know it comforts him. And, I know it comforts me.

"Look how far you've come, Charles. You walked fifty feet today! Last Friday, only a week ago, your legs couldn't bear weight and we didn't know if you would ever walk again. You are my warrior. You are courageous, and I am so proud of you."

"But," he says, "It's so hard. I'm so jealous of all the healthy bodies around me."

When it is almost too much, he talks in whispers. "Is it pain? Is it anxiety?" I ask. "Tell me, because we have a drug for each. How can I help you get comfortable?"

* * *

Friends make their favorite soup, beans, stew, and apple pie. They bring flowers, even medical marijuana. We have many more messages and acts of love and caring and support than we have the energy to acknowledge and respond with thanks.

Friends also drive Charlie to radiation, pick up prescriptions, take me to lunch, take Charlie to lunch when he is able, visit with him while I get a massage, and walk in and sit down at the exact moment when neither Charlie nor I can get up out of a chair.

* * *

The "Wheel of Fortune" Wheelmobile is in town to audition folks. I always thought it would be so outrageous to be chosen. I decide to audition and get out from under this heavy cloud. It is America's game show, you know.

"Are you ready to show us what you've got?" (Loud, wild applause and jumping up and down). On the spectrum of "Show us what you've got" to "What I really have," I realize how altered my life has become. This "Wheel of Fortune" will never give me what I need. Watching all this superficial fuss, I get bored and leave.

* * *

The hard news is that we have to postpone the next, long-term treatment therapies while Charlie's body heals from surgery and heals from radiation. The good news is that he is healing and is feeling better, just a little slower than we had hoped. Yesterday his appetite really came back and he was hungry! Second helpings followed by pie and ice cream.

* * *

Charlie and I have a bank account, an emotional bank account. When we are able to laugh and breathe freely, the account grows and we feel rich and in control. When we are sad and can't catch our breath, the account shrinks and we feel threatened and need to protect ourselves. Our account has been expanding and contracting a lot lately, shifting multiple times in one day. It's exhausting.

14

Suspense

*"If you arrive at a place in life that is miserable,
it will change, and something else about it will also be true."*
Almost Anything by Anne Lamott

"You're not dying," said the oncologist. "This is a very slow progressing disease and you may have two more years!"

We are stunned. Death is not imminent? Charlie can be pain free? There is still life to be lived? We leave the oncologist's office feeling soothed and hopeful.

* * *

Today is Saturday, a rest day. No physical therapy workouts, no radiation—quiet, no distractions. Time to get depressed for both of us as we absorb, observe, and evaluate all that has happened. Three months ago, last December, Charlie was riding his bicycle in Manhattan and South Florida. He was averaging 50 miles a week. Yes, he had a little pain, but who doesn't? Nothing he couldn't live with or complained about.

* * *

Mourning has begun. Our life as we knew it is irretrievably lost. And we each feel great sadness and mourn that our life as husband and wife is coming to an end. Already, how we live together is different, restructured. The future is full of uncertainty. What is it that we will need? How will we meet those needs?

Separate from 'we', I am ungrounded. My stomach is clenched, anxious, feeling tremendous change. What will my life be like?

We both recognize that we need to speak to a therapist.

Now, each day truly is a gift. We are exercising our spiritual muscles, grateful to have spent all these years practicing our faith. At this moment, life is difficult. I am resilient.

15

The Santa Fe Century Is Today!

"These and all things started as nothing, latent within a vast
energy-broth, but then we named them, and loved them, and,
in this way, brought them forth."
Lincoln in the Bardo by George Saunders

The Santa Fe Century is an annual one-hundred mile cycling event that attracts several thousand bicycle riders. Charlie loves the 'Century', as it is affectionately called. For the last five years he has been the Director, responsible for making sure all the details are complete and in place. Now, in a wheelchair, with very little energy and deteriorating steadily, he is still the Director. I pray it comes off without a glitch. Friends, family and lots and lots of volunteers are working to make it happen.

Jenne, our daughter, without being asked, silently has taken the reins and become an interim director. With great effort and energy, she has worked and is working to coordinate today's event and capture all the details, so next year we can do it again, as the 'Century' lives on.

The first wave of cyclists launch their one-hundred mile ride early, at 7 a.m. Always a chilly start, we bundle up and arrive on the scene by 6:30 a.m. So many people are happy to see us, to see Charles. I feel the energy swell.

* * *

I look and see Kieran, our son-in-law, over in the adjacent parking lot with friends preparing to ride and go to wish him safe journey.

"Good morning, Kieran," I say smiling. "Conditions couldn't be better. Blue sky. You might even have a tail wind."

"Good morning, Terre," he returns. "Where's Charlie?" I scan the venue and don't see him.

"Hmm. I don't know."

"Really, Terre? You lost a man in a wheelchair?"

"I guess I did."

* * *

There is a drone hovering over the hundreds of riders who have gathered at the start line behind the police escort. And there on the sideline is Charles, sitting in a prime position to watch the start, surrounded by close friends.

This year there are slightly more than 2,400 cyclists. The comments range from "flawless," to "awesome," and "the best

Century ever." So many people are being relied upon to follow through and do more of whatever is asked of them.

16

All at Once

"Stop trying to control the process."
Judy Tuwaletstiwa, Retrospective Exhibition
Santa Fe, New Mexico

Suddenly it's summer. The large, bright orange oriental poppies are blooming. The peonies are fragrant and happening. And the spring pansies are looking leggy and longing for shade and cooler weather.

And just as suddenly, everything falls apart.

Charlie's body is not handling the cancer drug. He has very low energy and is starting to sleep twenty hours a day. On Wednesday, we stop the cancer drug therapy. On Saturday, I take him to the emergency room. What we anticipate will be another average visit of six-to-seven hours in the ER turns into a hospital admission and a week.

Suddenly, it's the following Friday and together we make THE call. Treatments are not working. Charlie has begun hallucinating. It is time to go home.

Amazingly, the doctors appear: the primary care, the palliative care, and our medical oncologist. Individually, each sits with us in Charles' hospital room with the door closed and each concur that this is the appropriate decision. We just are not able to get ahead of the disease or buy enough time to allow the cancer drug therapy to work.

With great pain and many tears on my part, Charles is now home. For his part, he is calm, has no regrets, and no fear. If you speak with him, he will say he has had a good life.

17

Emotional Dilemma

"The imagery on the beautiful objects often reflected notions
of the physical and spiritual worlds as represented
through sophisticated patterns . . . which echo beliefs about
the inextricable relationship between these worlds."
Duality by Design by Paul Weidman

My mind is racing. Thinking. Thinking about the future, the cemetery. *Charlie, what kind of headstone do you want?* I won't ask him. This will be my decision.

And, "Are you going to put your name on it, too?" Asks my brother-in-law, Robert, with a smile.

I'm confused, overwhelmed. What do I want? I don't want dreary, sad, gray, that's for sure. I don't want to have to make these decisions. How is a stone the measure of a man?

* * *

I remember Charlie and I walking rows of graves in my family's ancestral cemetery and stopping and staring at my parents' headstone. There they were. They had even had a heart blasted between their names. I guess a stone can say anything, even lie.

"Hey, come here," Charlie said laughing. "Look at this. Sit on top of the stone and let me take your picture." I walk around and see my name on the back of their stone, as daughter. Implying what? We hadn't talked for more than 20 years prior to their death.

So, what do I want? I don't know who I am; how can I know what I want? I am not the daughter of those people. Soon, I will no longer be the wife of this man. I have never lived alone. I don't know how to move forward or what a life will look like without him.

18

Preparing Ourselves

"We were setting out on different roads.
The separation which is death itself."
A Grief Observed by C.S. Lewis

"Where Am I?"

"You're at home, Charlie, with me. In the library of the house you built for us. It is night, and what you are seeing is the reflection of the lamps in the windows of the doors to the sunroom. You are going to stay here with me, in our house, until your spirit leaves your body."

"What is happening?"

"You have cancer, Charlie. Your spirit is preparing to leave your body. Just like Michael, your son, and your mother and father, and all of your family who have already passed. Your spirit is going to be free of this broken body and you will be able to leave this bed."

"I'm afraid, Terre."

"Oh, I'm so glad you told me. If I were you, I would be afraid, too. I am here with you."

"When is this going to happen?"

"Soon, Charlie. Real soon. In the meantime, do you like the music playing on the radio? Is it loud enough? Can you hear it okay? Listen to the music and go back to sleep. I am here. I love you."

I love you, Charlie.

19

Peace

"The great paradox is that drawing nearer to death
will help begin to put it in the rear-view mirror.
Then, instead of living in conscious fear of its arrival,
crashing our party, we accept it as one of the musicians."
Almost Anything by Anne Lamott

We are now in the care of hospice.

The sense of urgency with which we have been living is gone. Gone also, are the drugs, the IVs, the blood draws, the doctor appointments, the anticipation, the worry, and the disappointment.

Charlie's spirit and some energy bounce back. Without pressure and no more drug side effects, each day now has real quality. He naps about an hour and a half mid-morning, and again in the afternoon.

So far, the confusion is very little and mostly happens for a short while when he is waking up. But when it happens, I feel a thud as we both have a reality check. Eventually, hallucinations will become dominant and the high calcium level will become lethal.

Charlie now leans on me and defers all decision making, asking only one promise: "Please, don't let me be in pain." I will do my best. We smile at each other a lot for reassurance. Each night we sing his family favorite oldies, but goodies:

A, You're Adorable

B, You're so Beautiful . . .

or

Let Me Call You Sweetheart,

I'm in Love with You . . .

I admit that I haven't been doing a very good job of taking care of myself. Sometimes I find I am holding my breath as if that would stop time. I don't care if I don't exercise; I don't care if I gain weight. I don't know how much time we have left together. I don't want to miss anything.

When I leave the house, I don't know what to do with myself. All I do is sit in the car and cry and cry and cry.

While I am gone, his brother and some friends decide to take Charlie out for lunch, for a burger and a beer. He really has no appetite, but it feels great to be out with the guys.

"Hey, Charlie, would you like a sip of my beer?"

For a moment, life feels almost normal. "To hell with a sip," says Charlie. "I'll have my own beer!"

20

Piercing the Veil

"Love and tender hearts carry the day."
Almost Anything by Anne Lamott

It's late, almost one in the morning; I am worn out. Charlie has not napped all day and will not go to sleep. Agitated and hallucinating, I cannot get him to settle. The medication he is on no longer seems to be working. Moving into the living room, I call the hospice nurse. The nurse tells me, "It's time to move to a stronger drug. It's time to start him on morphine. You have it as part of the drug package in your refrigerator."

"Morphine?" I repeat. "I have morphine in my refrigerator? You want me to start giving him morphine?"

She advises me on the dosage and the timing. "It's given orally, no shot. It's very easy to administer."

"Is this where we are now?" I am thinking. "I don't think I can. I want the nurse on call to come."

"Alright. I will put in the order. She will be there in about half an hour."

* * *

"Help me! Help me! Somebody. Please, help me!" Charlie shouts from his bed. As I rush in, I see him lying on his back with his legs dangling over the side rail. It looks as if he has been trying to get up.

"I'm here, Charlie," I say.

"Oh, good. Can you help me?"

"I believe I can," I respond as I go over to his legs.

"Be careful. You're going to have to take my shoes off first."

"I will. I can do it." Charlie is not wearing shoes. I go into a pantomime of untying and groaning as I tug at the first 'shoe'. "Got the first one," I say as I lift the leg up and gently set it down on the bed. I do the same thing with the second 'shoe'. "How's that?"

"Oh, that's great. Thanks a lot."

"You're welcome. Try closing your eyes."

As I am stepping out of the room he says, "My name is Charlie Loesch."

"Your name is Charlie Loesch?" I ask, turning and coming back to his bed.

"Yes," he nods.

Bending, with my face directly over his, I look into his eyes and say, "Well, guess what? My name is Terre Reed. Pleased to meet you. What do you say we get married? And, let's be married for about forty years. What do you say to that?"

A huge beautiful grin comes across his face. For a moment, I have pierced the veil.

21

Time Collapses

"For me, every hour is grace."
Eli Wiesel, Holocaust Survivor, Author
Nobel Peace Prize 1986

"It doesn't seem like I am getting any better," Charlie observes. "It seems like my body plateaus for a while, but really, I'm steadily getting worse. It feels like I'm on a slow downhill slide."

"I agree," I say. "It does look that way."

* * *

Death is sneaking up on us.

I thought we had several years.

Everyday Charlie wants to be outside on the couch under the portal in the courtyard. Even in the summer heat. "This is too hot for me," I say. It is after lunch; the temperature is rising, and the air is still.

His ability to walk is gone, but his upper body strength remains and he is able to help me transition him from the wheelchair to the car or couch or bed.

* * *

We are holding on.

I am sure we have months.

A few days later on a radiant Sunday morning, we have breakfast in the courtyard with friends. "You know," he realizes, "I am tired. I need to go into the house and take a nap. I want to lay down on my bed."

In the house, Charlie is too tired to assist me. I cannot lift him. Thankfully our guests are still here. Two men gently and swiftly move him onto the bed. It is mid-morning and I know he will never use his wheelchair again.

* * *

Time is collapsing.

Are we down to weeks?

That evening I realize this man is not sleeping. I call for help. The hospice nurse arrives. She stays until he has settled and is peaceful.

My personal power drains as I stand watch.

* * *

Death has given notice.

We have days.

I call our children and his brother and sister to tell them there has been a significant shift. I hold the phone to his ear so his sister, Betty, can speak directly to him.

"Charlie," she says, "Do you think you can wait until Friday?" Today is Monday. "I'm coming," she says, "but our flight is not until Friday. Please wait."

"I don't know," is his whisper.

When she hangs up, he sadly looks at me, "I don't know if I can wait that long."

Then, with recognition he says quietly, "It's really happening, isn't it Terre? I'm dying, aren't I?"

"Yes, you are," is all I can say.

His eyes glisten as tears form and find their way down his cheeks. He weeps. He mourns. His body shakes with grief, not because he is dying, but because he knows that we are near the end. This is good-bye.

* * *

Death holds all the power.

Now I am aware. We are down to hours.

From then on, he mostly sleeps. He wakes for a few moments when family members arrive. Finally, he has no more energy. It is too much to speak or open his eyes.

Surrounded by family, surrounded by love, we try to hold on. Standing at his bedside, I bend and place my head on his shoulder, in the curve of his neck, my arm across his chest. His body is warm. Alive.

When I start to cramp, I have to stand up. Turning my head, I look out the window. "Mom!" My daughter shouts. Turning, I see Charlie's arm straight up in the air, his hand reaching. I take it. I hold it. I kiss it. This is our last communication.

* * *

We have surrendered.

There are only minutes.

He is a good brother. He waits for his sister.

"Let's sing a song," I say, as we all gather around him. Betty leads us in an old Irish ditty that their mother would sing at the ocean, at night, with everyone sitting around a roaring summer beach fire:

"Bridgette O'Flynn, Bridgette O'Flynn

Where have you been?

'Tis a fine time for you to come in.

You been to the parade, O' the parade me eye.

Never did a parade take so long in passing by . . . ."

As always, at the end of the song, we are all smiling at each other. At that very moment, Charles opens his eyes wide, looking at someone or something we cannot see. We are witnessing his spirit leaving his body. I hold his head, placing one hand on each cheek. "I love you Charles! Good-bye Charles. Go with God."

* * *

With the help of family, we bathe him. We dress him. I sit in silence with his body. I remove my wedding ring.

Now, I am empty. Now, I am nothing.

I am left behind. Our time together is complete.

Part Two
Transition

What Happened?
Terre Reed
August, 2019
30" x 36"
Oil on Canvas

To view this painting in color, go to
TerreReed.com

99

22

Missing You

"Grief is praise, because it is the natural way
love honors what it misses."
The Smell of Rain on Dust by Martin Prechtel

My Dear Maestro,

I've been waiting. Waiting for you to talk to me. Waiting for a dream, a sign, or an outright communication. We already told each other what was in our hearts. We had the opportunity to say good-bye. Now, you're gone.

* * *

Do you know how hard it is?

Like jumping off a boat, without stopping and every part of my body screaming, I have plunged in fully dressed. Your ashes and flowers already drifted away.

* * *

I will move my easels into your shop. I will keep your tools and let your overalls hang on their peg awhile longer. Your work boots sit under a bench. How else can I keep you close?

It's so much easier to keep working on your life than mine. Being solo feels like I've lost my overcoat, like the ballast of my ship is gone. But I have e-mails to answer, calls to return, choices to make, friends and family who tell me they love me.

* * *

My garden carries on without me. Volunteer morning glories climb volunteer sunflowers. Tomatoes, peppers, and kale decide to grow on their own, waiting for me to reclaim them.

* * *

We both knew from the start that our relationship had a beginning, a middle, and end.

There never really is enough time, is there?

Love Always

23

Adrift

"No matter what, you have to find a way for the grief
of your loss to turn into life again."
The Smell of Rain on Dust by Martin Prechtel

Strangers on the news cry, "I've lost everything . . . . " In hurricane, fire, catastrophe. "I have to start over." What they mean is that they have to start rebuilding the things they have lost.

I've lost something else that cannot be rebuilt, something intangible, something inside of me. I've lost myself. My life as I knew it has been so shattered, there is no way Humpty Dumpty can be put back together again.

Start over? I can't start over. This is death. My life as it was when Charles was alive is so completely gone that, it too, is dead.

I knew myself. I knew who I was. I stood on firm ground. I had edges. Definition. And, I liked my life. But now, more than losing Charles, *MY* life is gone. The comfort of routine, plans, familiarity, structure, and continuity—all gone. As I sit and rock back and forth, feeling my pain, the pain of separation, trying to sort things out, the magnitude of this very personal loss in addition to losing Charles continues to hit me.

Loss is emptiness, a void. Space is created. Frightening space. And loneliness and lack. Without the cloak of definition, I am weak and vulnerable.

I look around and see others who have lost their spouses, their lives. Some move to be closer to their children; some move in with them. Some throw themselves into their work or immerse themselves in volunteering. Some start dating immediately and remarry quickly. Some say they are still married, but their spouse is in heaven, waiting. Some visit psychics or mediums in an attempt to keep the relationship going.

I thrash around for solutions. "Don't move too fast, Terre," Charlie had said. "Take a year to let things settle." I promise I will and now I am.

So, the first thing is—I do nothing. Every day my emotional loss appears to grow as I assess how every single aspect of my life is affected. There're only my clothes in the laundry basket. Sure is quiet around here. I withdraw. I shut down.

I go deeper into myself. I am wounded. I want to hide. Life feels negative. Like a clean countertop that invites clutter, I silently beg for the emptiness to be filled. This emptiness that feels like so much weight.

Lacking confidence, I experience the utmost sadness. These feelings only propel me lower. When I see friends, I make no effort to conceal my pain. One day it dawns on me that in their compassion they are reflecting my misery back to me. "Oh, you poor thing," one person mirrors perfectly. "You poor, poor, thing. I don't know how you do it. It's just so sad."

That's what I am, a poor thing? It's come to this? If that is who I am, then I am a big disappointment to myself. Whether it's a reaction or a response, I stack my bones, and stand up tall. From now on, I am fine. I am trying. I am working through grief. I am healing. I smile when greeted. And people respond in kind. Change comes from within.

24

Filling the Void

"When we suffer loss, we have to learn to heal and learn to be
generous with whatever has caused us to heal.
That is what turns grief into life and beauty."
The Smell of Rain on Dust by Martin Prechtel

A silent energy flowed between Charlie and me. There was a deep, unseen, unspoken power and empowerment that developed over the years. I could relax in the security of this love; that was our relationship.

My love for Charles remains in the present tense, for which I am grateful. But now his humanness is gone. So, what do I do with this love that still continues? This love, like downed power lines sizzling and flapping, is alive and disconnected.

My body is in pain. Why is life still continuing as if nothing has happened? "Stop!" I want to scream. "The world needs to stop and acknowledge the magnitude of what just happened!" I can't go on. I want to shut down. I want to withdraw. I can't take it in.

The holes in my life seem so conspicuous and raw. How do I begin to heal? How can I comfort myself?

* * *

Our marriage did have rocks. Both of us were willful and opinionated. So, from time to time we got a tune up. Once, when we were at odds, the counselor gave us homework. Each night, in bed, before we fell asleep, we were to say three things we appreciated about the other. No matter what. No matter if we hadn't seen each other or didn't have warm feelings at that moment. This became a habit. We always fell asleep feeling somewhat appreciated.

I miss that ritual. So, I'm going to say three things out loud that I enjoyed about today. It doesn't have the same impact, but it's something. Then, my therapist changes the ritual, "Say out loud three things you did for yourself—three things you did that showed appreciation for yourself today."

Much harder. Today, I actually made a meal. Today, I went outside. Today, I listened to my body and took a nap.

'Compassion' has new value in my vocabulary. This ritual is the beginning of compassion for myself. I acknowledge my loss; my heart is greatly softened. I see I am still here.

Learning to be gentle with myself and to appreciate myself is learning how to love myself. Some of the energy I have for Charles, is redirected back to me. As I do this for myself, my view of the world and my attitude toward life is more gentle, more compassionate. This is the beginning of healing.

25

I Am Lost

"Bardo refers to that state in which we have lost our
old reality and it is no longer available to us."
"The Four Essential Points of Letting Go"
by Pema Khandro Rinpoche

As I tried to brace myself and prepare for the death of my husband, another death was sneaking up on me—my own. I had no idea that with his death, I would also experience the death of my life as I had known it.

Saying good-bye to Charles is the saddest, most painful experience I have ever had. I can never think about his death without touching my pain, my sadness. It remains the lowest, most empty, broken point of my life. And yet, I am still here.

I knew myself. I knew who I was in the world. My life had structure, continuity. Not anymore. Abruptly, all aspects, all levels of living shattered.

Priorities aren't priorities. All goals are irrelevant. Nothing looks the same. I don't look the same. Time is meaningless. My house, my home, is empty and unfamiliar.

Buddhists define the period of time after death and before rebirth as the Bardo. I know now, I, too, have died. I have died a living death and have entered my Living Bardo. I have suffered a loss so great, so traumatic that my old identity is gone. Moving forward I am a different, yet unknown person.

What is it that saves me? What is it that keeps me from surrendering my life to this awful situation? The only answer I can think of is: Life. I am a voyager on a world that keeps turning and takes me with it. I hate it when friends, well intended, say, "You'll feel better in time. Give it time." Or, "You'll get through this. You are a strong woman and you'll get through this. Just wait." Neither time nor strength has gotten me through.

Simply, if you're not one thing then you're something else. If you're not married, then you're single. If your husband died, then you are a widow. And so a new life begins, ready or not.

26

I Am Responsible

"I think I am beginning to understand
why grief feels like suspense.
It comes from the frustration of so many impulses
that had become habitual."
A Grief Observed by C.S. Lewis

In the early morning sun, I sit in the rocker in the kitchen. The day is so full of potential. I just don't know what to do with myself. Where is everybody? The aloneness that I feel now is so much more vast than the aloneness at any other time in my life.

In the past, I experienced being by myself for weeks at a time, for months even. But I always knew there was connection. There would be a coming home. Sitting in this rocker, I am waiting for him. Tell me about your day. What do you want to do about dinner?

I can't stand it. I want to run away, mostly from myself. I want to climb out of my skin and be somebody else. Is the universe trying to teach me a lesson? Or is it punishing me?

I promise my therapist that I will sit still for twenty minutes every day. Sit still and just breathe. Just be. Allow the feelings. Allow the tears. Allow the sadness to seep out. I am changed. The sadness tenderizes me, takes away my drive. As much as I am uncomfortable with uncertainty, now I don't care. The sadness has become a part of me.

"Let it teach you," says my therapist. "Be with it. Be gentle with yourself. You are learning compassion."

Weeks go by.

Slowly I realize that part of accepting his death is accepting that I am responsible for my own happiness. After sitting for twenty minutes I acknowledge my feelings, and then, I live my day.

27

What Do I Do?

"Your vision will become clear only when you can look into
your own heart. Who looks outside, dreams;
who looks inside, awakes."
Letters, Vol.1, by Dr. Carl Jung

5 a.m.

I have no water! There is no running water!

I must leave in two hours to catch the 7:13 a.m. train to
the airport to begin my trek east with your ashes.

There are three other houses besides mine on this well.
Three other houses occupied with my tenants. I am now alone
and solely responsible.

I need help. I'm not going into that dark abyss of a below
ground well house by myself. It frightens me and I wouldn't
know what I was looking at. It's too early to call anyone.

Breathe. Please. Help.

Finish packing. No shower, no doing my hair. Wash my
face and brush my teeth with bubble water.

* * *

I text the tenants telling them that I am aware the well is out and I'm on it. Ha!

Who is the well guy, anyway? Where is our copy of the list of emergency contacts you left with the tenants while we were away last summer?

Rummaging through the catch-all drawer of miscellaneous papers, I sigh with relief. Got it. Aurora Pump and Well. Talk to Bob.

Calling, the answering machine picks up. "Hi, this is Bob. We are gone for the Labor Day weekend, but if this is an emergency, you can call Joaquin at . . . ."

This isn't working. All I am doing is leaving messages.

Leave? Is this what someone who is in charge does? Get on a train?

You seemed to handle worrying so well, Charlie. Maybe that's why you got on your bicycle and rode for miles. Me? What am I going to do? It's too early for ice cream, and sugar doesn't calm the ache inside anymore.

On the train I reach out to my friend, David. It's still so early; I leave yet another message. At last, David calls back. "Do you think you could go down into the well house and have a look around?" I ask. "See if a circuit blew or something? Thank you, so much."

* * *

I am checked in and at the gate waiting, waiting. I practice my breathing and try to let the adrenaline flow out of me.

I did not cancel my plans because you wouldn't have. You would have kept going. Isn't that right, Charles?

My phone rings. David is laughing. Problem solved. Water is back on. A large black stink bug was trapped in a flapper valve trying to close. Lifting up the flapper, the bug, still alive, was free to move on and the valve could close, triggering the pump. We have water!

Deep exhale. With help, I did it. Problem solved. No more crisis. I can do this.

Drained. I stand and prepare to board my flight. I pick up my carry-on, the wooden box containing your ashes, and realize for the first time they weigh about twenty pounds.

28

Before and Now

My Memory

"Pain is always a sign we are holding onto something –
usually ourselves."
Uncomfortable with Uncertainty
by Pema Chodron

"You know, I could go first." I would say that when the topic
of death came up.

"Well, statistics say that men usually die first and I am
ten years older," would be his response. "Realistically, I'm
probably going first, Terre."

* * *

We had lively discussions about the parameters of our
long-term commitment to each other and created a written
agreement. Three main tenets stood out:

First: This relationship is voluntary. Meaning, don't give me your @#$%&! No one is allowed to come home frustrated and take it out on the other person.

Second: If the relationship is not working, we agree to see it to its conclusion before entering into another relationship. We both had been married before and carried some hurts.

Third: The relationship is finite. Just as it has a beginning, it will have an end.

And, it was a surprise ending indeed. Oh, how I wish I had gone first. Then I wouldn't be the one that is left with an aching missing heart.

For years we slept in a double bed where it's impossible not to touch. You could turn your back and scoot to the edge, so close you would be about to fall off. But sooner or later, there would be a soft bump, a warm touch, a draping of an arm, a reaching out somewhere, somehow, making it impossible to fall asleep angry.

But now you are gone, and the bed is empty.

I thought I had a plan. You knew that I loved you. When I realized you were dying, I tried to love you with all my heart. My plan was that after you passed, I would feel no regrets and the healing would be easier. Now you are gone, and I have no regrets. But my heart hurts like hell.

29

Struggle Redux

"Some of us grew up in alternative unhappy marriages, where we accepted as normal disparate parental need."
Almost Anything by Anne Lamott

Charlie died and I am now broken. I have now retreated back to the first things I learned in childhood. I have no self-esteem, no self-confidence. I am lost, abandoned and slide into depression.

As an adult, I get to handle shame, codependency, and unworthiness all over again. Not only do I get to remember, I get to relive these crippling childhood states of mind.

* * *

Thanks, dad. You held all the power, didn't you? Permission, affection, and harmony in our house depended on your mood. You hurt me. You said you were protecting me. You said it was for my own good. I was afraid of you. Over time

I got the unworthy, unlovable, who do you think you are messages. I had to fight for myself, fight my way back. Because, if I didn't, then you would win.

But you didn't win. Not back then, not today. The core strength I developed as a child out of the need to survive is still inside me. I am strong.

* * *

Today, I fight again; not angrily this time but determinedly, doggedly. I know what I have to do. I have won before and I will win again.

I learn anew about self-care and self-love. I try to be the most beautiful woman I can be, inside out, growing spiritually, expanding my self-awareness. I learn again how to comfort myself. I am able to access the mystic chords of my memory and recall positive experiences, great moments with good laughs.

I am winning!

30

Emptiness

"One of the hardest gates to pass through is the gate of acceptance:
I am here; I am alive; I am now."
"Hero with a Thousand Faces,"
NPR interview with Joseph Campbell

In a restaurant at dinner last night, I found myself staring at the chair on the other end of my table. The couples, on either side of me were smiling and engaging one another with the joy that comes from meeting new, interesting people. For me, they were backdrop, a bubbling brook of conversation, while I connected with the detail of that empty chair.

Today, I sit by the large window in his woodworking shop. The sun pours in and warms this cold space. I see a beautiful peach rose blooming out of the window. I hear the second hand on the clock ticking, myself breathing, and the pen scratching on the paper. I hear a bird chirping. Insistently. It has something to tell.

I look around and see what's waiting to get done. It waits and I write. I am in that suspension where I don't want to forget, and yet I need new memories and experiences—not to replace but to ease the process of losing and fill the aloneness.

The mess I see is my mess, and whatever needs doing has to be my doing. The large shop air compressor kicks on. I must have forgotten to turn it off. No one does that for me. Now the freezer kicks on. It, too, has an air compressor; this one freezing, the other one blowing blasts of air. And then, there are the compressors on the roof of the walk-in coolers Charlie had designed and built.

How did it get to be October? How did it get to be fall? How is it he has been gone now 15 weeks? Almost four months. Time is racing and the space between us seems to be growing wider and wider. His absence is still very new . . . no time at all.

My thoughts consume me. I cannot tell you what they are. Perhaps like dreams, when I return to the present, they are gone. A dear friend walks in the door as I fold towels. "Did I know you were coming?" I vaguely remember a phone call.

My friends are loving me and setting me down gently. They reach out to me. They want to spend time with me. "How are you?" is the relentless question. I lack words to describe how I am. "Okay," seems to be the only word that comes out of my limited vocabulary.

How did I get multiple tissue boxes and a roll of paper towels on my desk? In fact, tissue boxes are in every room, everywhere I look. Sitting in his shop, now my space, the last of my company gone, I feel myself sinking as I continue to drain.

It's time to feel my own edges. I don't know where I begin or end. Taking time for me, my intention is immediate. I feel supported as I pick the peach rose and trim the rosehips off the bush, giving it my full attention. I notice shoulder muscles slightly relax, notice thoughts, maybe notice some feeling.

A hawk has visited several times. Swooping over the roof of the portal, she lands on a *piñon* branch on the other side of the courtyard wall. She sits there watching, waiting, alone. Perhaps she is my role model.

31

Mornings Are the Easiest,
Evenings Are the Hardest

"I am myself and my circumstances."
Some Lessons in Metaphysics, by Jose Ortega y Gassett

In the evening, tired and alone, if I am not careful, Grief will
come and sit down beside me. Grief is shock and impact. Grief
is real pain. Grief is only thinking about myself and how small
I am. Without Charles as my partner, I feel so limited.

Life and death. Or, love and loss. Or, love and grief. I
have spent my life on the loving part. Now I am aware how
little experience I have with deep loss and death. I know it is a
part of life. But in the wonderful juicy moments and in the
hard, struggling moments, I would guess no one is thinking
about death as a part of life.

Where is there the least amount of pain? Hanging out in
memories of the past takes me into a darkness. I should be
able to handle this. But I am not. An antidepressant has been
a life jacket that keeps my head above water.

What am I afraid of? Fear of the future. Can I handle it? Will I have to move? Can I take care of the things he took care of? Can I take care of myself? I see mystery, uncertainty, and unknowns. So many changes, I have lost my structure. There is no continuity. I envision myself as an egg whose shell has cracked and broken. How do I roll without a shell?

It is only because he is not here that I am forced to work so intensely on myself. The process starts with, "What am I going to do now? Charlie was a large presence, so a lot of space has been created. How am I going to fill it? And by the way, who am I anyway as I enter this next new period of my life?"

So where is that place with the least amount of pain? I find it in the present moment. It is the safest and most soothing place I can be.

And how do I roll without a shell? Trust—with my eyes open. Who do I trust? How do I trust? When do I trust?

Trust myself. Above all, trust myself.

32

Reframing Myself

"His grief unnerved him, and made him a weak, passive child.
I did not dream his rugged nature could be so moved."
Lincoln in the Bardo by George Saunders

There has been a rupture, a seismic break with the past. What remains are memories, skills, preferences, and habits. I agree that I am who I am today largely because of who I was in the past and who I was with Charlie.

He insulated me. I lived in a world where there were chores and parts of my life that I didn't think about. Like how much gas was in the car or did I have enough cash. With Charlie being a builder, I never hesitated to ask him to make something or hang a picture or help solve a problem. His response was always swift, immediate, and seemingly effort-less.

I succeeded in my careers with ambition, making things happen. Now I have no drive and the idea that I allow life to evolve, unfold, and come to me is alien. How do I create a life that gives me more than survival?

It is so tempting to rush and just fill space. This is my conundrum. I must be receptive. I watch. I see that I am the one who has to change, who has to be different. My heart is pummeled and softened. I don't want the pain and loneliness to continue. I want a more interesting, more fun, and more satisfied me.

The old contrived self has been rather rudely emptied out. As if someone, in this case an event, has gone into my closet and thrown out everything—the old, never wear again stuff and the new dress with tags still on, that I had been looking forward to wearing. Out also went motivation and goals. There is now an empty closet and I am naked. We all have a soft underbelly; mine is exposed.

Sitting in a corner, slightly beaten up, one thing has remained—my personality. I'm still here. I take a serious unadorned look at myself. I have lost a lot, but I am not injured. Independent of another, I start to take mental note of what I like about myself, what I prefer, and what I want for myself. This is the beginning of my process of increased self-awareness. This is part of my Living Bardo.

More than thirty-five years ago, Charlie's son, Michael, died. We were swamped in grief. Someone said, "You know there is joy in every moment. You just have to choose it." Then and now, I would like to smack that person. However, the comment has stayed, challenging me. I notice that not every moment is painful. There is humor in the absurd. And what was normal before can be absurd now.

When I revisit the last days of Charlie's life, I see smiles and humor. His hallucinations were pretty wild and outrageous, not awful. Living life with the awareness of impermanence is a good reason to look for humor and laugh at my own jokes.

Knowing I'm still here is empowering. Empowering to take risk, to acknowledge what I already know from life's experience. I want to create my new world with a light heart and a playful attitude. As Charlie would say, "Grab life by the handlebars!"

Part Three
Renewal

Ghost Tree
Terre Reed
July, 2019
30" X 36"
Oil on Canvas

To view this painting in color, go to
TerreReed.com

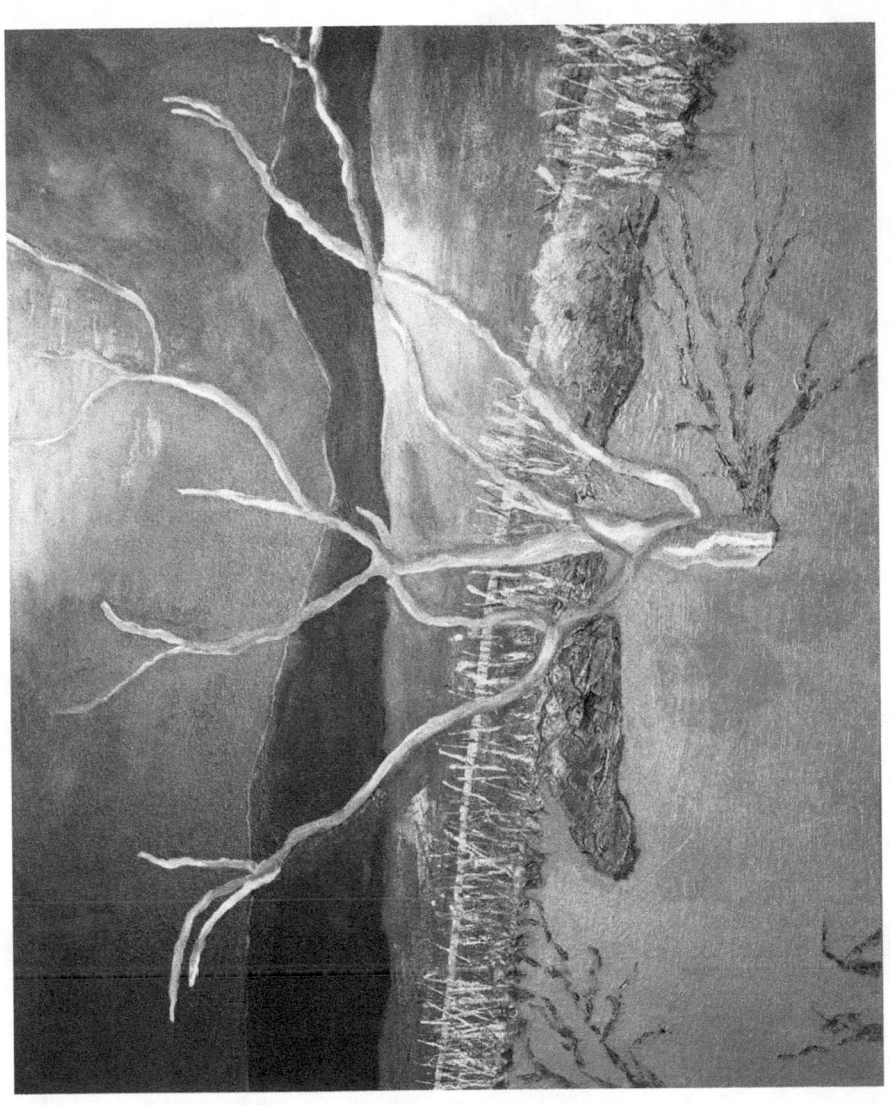

33

Understanding the Process

"That we therefore do have the potential
to view our experience more insightfully,
is a powerful method of releasing us
from the dissonant and perhaps even fearful qualities
of our own-self-made, perceptual landscape."
The Tibetan Book of the Dead Introduction by HH Dalai Lama

I am not the first person to lose a husband. For thousands of years humans have been giving birth, living, and dying. Whether I am a cave woman, a war widow in ancient Greece, or someone who has lost their husband to cancer today the same pain and sorrow is immediate. How do they cope? Then and now.

I am curious and fascinated with parallels in myth, ancient history, tribes, and current religions. Many include stories of death, transition, and rebirth. Or in Christian terms: Crucifixion, Transformation, and Resurrection. Or in Buddhist terms: Death, Bardo, and Rebirth.

I read numerous books in the "loss and recovery" genre. Anytime someone makes a suggestion, I read it. I enjoy Joseph Campbell's series on PBS, "The Power of the Myth." I also read *The Tibetan Book of the Dead*. Buddhists believe in reincarnation and this book addresses the time between death and rebirth called the Bardo. Then, I observe how this process, this 'cycle of existence', includes me.

I notice patterns of loss that I have lived through many times in my life, some daily, some incidental and some tragic. Mostly, I have not been paying attention. I see how impermanent life is! How quickly things can and do change! Feeling the results of my loss so acutely, I witness how loss, transition, and renewal repeat continually.

I have not died a literal death, but my life as I knew it has; I am in a Living Bardo. Learning to heal and care for myself becomes my transformation. Similarly, how I reshape my life and move forward becomes my renewal.

* * *

I am beginning to understand that my view of the world only exists in my mind. My perspective is colored by emotions, moods, history, experience, and what is happening in the moment. And once again, as I was taught when I sought help dealing with my thoughts as a result of an abusive childhood, I am taught that comfort, healing, validation, affirmation, confidence, and happiness come from within.

I lunch with my pastor who has had years of sitting with the dying and comforting the survivors. I ask, "In grief, what questions do other Christians ask?" I want to know that I am not alone. To my surprise, one of the most frequently asked questions is, "Why did this happen?" They, too, are trying to understand and process their experience.

I asked this question early in Charlie's illness, already knowing the answer. No one knows why. It just is. And with this irreversible diagnosis, my life as I knew it started to dissolve. As I look back, mourning subtly began then.

I also asked him if it was true that some people stop going to church after they have lost a spouse. "Yes," is his answer.

"Why do you think that is?" I ask.

"Because they are mad at God. Or, they feel abandoned by God."

I do not feel abandoned or let down. I go to church because I believe in God, or God Energy, or maybe it's just habit. The serenity and peacefulness I experience there does comfort me.

As long as I continue to look for comfort in the past, I suffer. When I stop asking why did this happen and start asking how am I going to heal, life begins to shift.

Stepping Out

"It is undeniably the case in our society we do not easily accept death as a part of life, which results in a perpetual sense of insecurity and fear . . ."
The Tibetan Book of the Dead Introduction by HH Dalai Lama

I always wanted laugh wrinkles.

We are going to wrinkle up, that's a given. So why not choose what kind of wrinkles we get? I look in the mirror and I am surprised by what I see. When did I get that frown line?

Of course, in the sadness, I don't smile.

I was vivacious; I was fearless. Was. Was I that way because of me or because I had an unspoken safety net? I was free to take risk, try new things, try new ideas. We took care of each other. We were there for each other.

What's going to happen to me now that he's gone? Who will look out for me? Who will help me and be there for me? We shared stories at the end of our day. We shared our lives. Now what?

As a child, to protect myself, I would stand very still and hold my breath, hoping not to get noticed, hoping not to get hit. I was very frightened. I practiced this technique for years.

I am back to being invisible. I am frightened. I have to remind myself to breathe. It's easy to hide, to stay home and not be noticed.

When I can't stand the loneliness, the lack of companionship and connection, I go to the grocery. I buy food without a plan or sense of quantity. I am embarrassed to ask the butcher for one pork chop. I don't want him to know that I am alone. I watch people shop. "How are you today?" asks the checkout clerk. I come back to a silent house. I throw out a lot of food.

For months I think, what can I do with myself, by myself? What is the little something that I might enjoy with others which would allow me to be seen, but still be anonymous? I don't want to say that "I am single," and I cannot say the words: "I am a widow."

I go to church, a church I've never been to before. The ritual and familiarity are soothing. I can be seen, yet not feel exposed. I don't want them to know my story.

Friends include me in dinner parties and poker nights. I don't like being the only single person there. It heightens my rawness, my aloneness. I need to find opportunities to go into the community and still feel safe.

I join a writing group that meets once a month. We share first names. The leaders give us prompts and we write for fifteen minutes. Then, they announce that we will go around the room, each person reading what they have written. I feel very embarrassed to share my thoughts aloud and am so relieved when it's over. To my surprise, I am given positive feedback. They accept my efforts. I feel I belong. I am now part of a new group.

Reading the newspaper, I see dance lessons advertised on Sunday afternoons at a nearby dance studio. No partner needed. I love to dance. But that's not something Charlie would do, and I wouldn't do it without him. The reminder that he is no longer here comes once again. But this time, a realization occurs to me. I am free to take these lessons. They might be fun, if I can get up the courage to walk through the door.

What's the worst that could happen? I suffer through an hour and never go back? After a few weeks, I talk myself into going. This is a risk that I am willing to take.

Salsa. They are teaching introduction to salsa this afternoon. Each person introduces themself. We stand in a circle without a partner and practice the steps without music. At the end of the class, the instructor puts on some slow salsa and we are all smiling and dancing!

As I leave, I feel a boost in energy. A tiny piece of myself has come back.

35

Who Am I Now?

"Life is what we are and what we do;
it is, then of all things the closest to each one of us.
Put a hand on it and it will let itself be grasped like a tame bird."
Some Lessons in Metaphysics by Jose Ortega y Gasset

My definition of 'widow' is that I do not stand alone. As in the old western movies, "Ole' Widda' Loesch. Ya' know, she's got five hundred head of cattle over thar'. Someone ought'a talk to her; make a deal." I am never just 'widow.'

So, I am Charlie's widow. There is a certain left over security in that. When I drive Big Red, men approach me, "How much you want for that truck?" It is incongruous to them that I should have this old red truck. Or, folks ask, "How's Charlie's truck doing? Call me. I'd be happy to take it off your hands." Yes, for a long time it was Charlie's truck. But now it's my truck. At first it did feel foreign to be driving it, but now I've taken ownership. I consider it one of the gifts he left me.

I am proud to have been his wife. But as long as I refer to myself as his widow I am still leaning on him, on the relationship. It's not that I move out of widowhood, I'll always be Charlie's widow. Instead, it is that I move more into myself.

Losing Charlie created huge space in my life. Staying in grief is how I honored him, how I appreciated and saw the huge impact of him on my life. Separation is painful. Feeling raw, I now see more clearly the little deaths we all experience daily. Along with those little good-byes, I see that I am forced to make choices all by myself. This is how life pulls me along.

I have a hole in my fabric. I have undefined space that was his. In addition, I now have my own undefined life. In short, there is nothing to grasp, nothing to hold onto. How I fill this emptiness is the next chapter of my life.

I like being tired at the end of the day. It means that I have done something versus sitting and staring into space which I have done and then cannot sleep. With the help of my therapist, I notice how mood affects my energy level and my perception.

I am guided to see that as I make choices, I am slowly reshaping and reinventing myself. Pain is a motivator. I do not want to remain in the intense pain that goes with loss and grief. I want to heal.

I change because I have been changed; my life being so different now. At some point I choose a willingness to change. That is the fulcrum of my Living Bardo, my transition—that point where I stop being pulled and start reaching for new life.

I accept that I am alive, and I want to fully experience what that means. Slowly, I set intentions. I make choices. I invite friends and new people into my life. Using Charlie's death as a baseline, I am willing to take some risk. I see what brings me joy.

Moving along, willingly or not, on this continuum of life I move further away from widowhood. How do I define myself now? By the choices I make. Who am I? I am alive and I fully want to experience what that means.

Will I see Charlie again? I don't know. That's part of the mystery. I know that I experience him within me. When I think about him, I feel his energy and it comforts me.

Today, I introduce myself as "Terre." That's it, no back story. As you get to know me you will eventually learn that I was married and my husband died. It will not be the first thing you learn, because who I am takes precedence over who we were.

I know that life has pain. Through the loss of who and what I held very dear—I know pain. Yet, I say "yes" to life and all its pain because joy is also on the same continuum. And that continuum is love.

Go Ahead and Flirt ...

"One need to fully experience an emotion in order to detach from it.
Like lust, loneliness and fear."
Romeo and Juliet by William Shakespeare

"I am ashamed. I did something. I know better, but I did it anyway. All of the conditions of my PTSD were triggered, and I jumped. And, I willingly put myself in a potentially dangerous situation," I said holding back tears.

"Alright, Terre. Tell me. What have you done now that you haven't already done in your life?" asked my therapist, smiling.

"I slept with someone. From the start there were red flags. I mean, from very early in our first conversation, and I ignored all of them. He seemed so playful, fun, and smart. I laughed. I felt adrenaline, thrill, risk, some illicitness, and went for it. And the sex, by the way, was not fun. It was very disappointing, which probably was a good thing because it helped break the spell." With relief I said all of this out loud.

"Focus on your breath, Terre. Just sit quietly for one minute and focus on your breath. Eyes open. Now, what exactly are you ashamed of?"

"I hold two keys. One is to my house and one is to my body. I don't let just anyone in. And here, without hesitation, within minutes, I allow this man, this stranger to slide into my most intimate inner circle. I can't have that. I'm not safe. I need to know what I can do to protect myself so that this doesn't happen again."

"Stay with your breath. Right now, be with your breath. In all things, go back to your breath. If you had been able to go back to your breath just for a moment or two before you leapt, do you think you would have made different decisions?"

"I don't know. Possibly. But I was blindsided. We were just smiling and chatting, enjoying the Holiday lights on the Plaza when he took my hand. For a moment I was stunned. It felt so good to be holding hands. No one has held my hand in a long time. I did not let go. Then, a short while later, he put his arm around my waist and pulled me close. I felt such a heat rush. It felt wonderful, irresistible. I wanted those feelings to continue."

"Stay with your breath."

"I know I am in deficit. It's hard not having closeness and intimacy in my life. I really miss it. But I accept that it's not happening today. I put those feelings in a box for now. I put them on a shelf. He gets to that box in an instant, throws open the lid, and all those pent-up feelings come out!"

"It doesn't work that way, Terre. You can't do that. You can't put feelings in a box on a shelf. It's all energetics. It's all part of you and who you are. You are going to have to learn how to use those energies in your daily life."

"I don't understand. I have been trying so hard to live consciously, think before I speak and act. Be present. I know that my life is flat right now, there is no magic. But I accept that as part of the grief process."

"No, no, no, Terre. You know what adrenaline is. Now use it. You can give yourself a high, a rush, whenever you want. Serve yourself portions daily. Everyday. Life's too short. Have fun. Take some risk. Try new things. Put yourself out there. Go ahead and flirt, be playful, enjoy yourself! But in portions when you want, when you decide."

"I'm not sure I know how to do that."

"Experiment. Look for opportunities and give yourself some of this feel good adrenaline in small amounts at first. Relax. You are learning; you are growing. Your self-awareness is increasing. Now, I think you are ready for some deep work. We'll start next week."

"I thought I was doing 'deep work'. What are you talking about?"

"Worthiness."

Your Things

"An image can be a transformative gift of healing."
Judy Tuwaletstiwa, Retrospective Exhibition
Santa Fe, New Mexico

The thought of removing anything of yours feels like I am erasing you. But then it gets ridiculous. After six months or so in this Southwest climate, I notice the shoulders on your undisturbed clothes hanging in the closet are dusty, showing your absence. It is better to have them gone. Gone? Well, bagged and put in the downstairs closet for now.

And that commanding portrait of you over the fireplace. You loved that painting and would never allow it to hang anywhere else. In it, you are looking directly at me, about to break into a smile. One day I realized that I was talking to that damn painting. Not just talking to it, but crying to it, dancing in front of it and having a one-sided conversation. Okay, that's it. It has to go. There is only one person here now. No, I didn't throw it out. It is carefully stored, waiting for its next iteration.

Did you really leave me your woodworking shop to dismantle? The shop you had for thirty-five years? For almost a year, I let it be, looking like it was waiting for you to return. You were a stasher. You liked to store things in every nook and cranny. When a shelf got full, you built a new one out of scrap wood. Did you know you had thirty pounds of screws in every shape, size, color, and purpose in little boxes covered with a fine yellow flour of sawdust?

If I don't dismantle it, this place will become a mausoleum. I learn more about you as I discover, inventory, sort, throw out, give away, and make ready to sell. Slow and painful, I am good for about an hour and a half before I hit an emotional wall. Going back into the house, I lay on the couch and stare at the ceiling for a couple of hours. At this rate, it will take forever.

One morning I wake up and a little voice in my head says, "You know, Terre, that shop would make a great studio." What? I flew out of bed and stood in my jammies in the middle of your space. This could be the best studio ever!

"Well, you know," continued the voice, "If you make it your studio, you have to work. You have to use it; you can't just leave it sit." Yes, I know. I know. I will.

The energy begins to flow. And a transformation begins in earnest. I ask for help. We give away most of the small power tools, and in an afternoon sell all of the big machinery. I don't know what the long-term use of this space will be; but for now, I know that I must be the first to use it. I have to take ownership. The most painful, awful, wonderful gift I have ever received.

38

My Experience Is My Life

"Define color in terms of memory and emotion."
Judy Tuwaletstiwa, Retrospective Exhibition
Santa Fe, New Mexico

Life is simple. I spend a lot of time alone. This new me is slowly being shaped by self-reflection in my alone time and by the small choices I make on a daily basis.

Another gentle, subtle, shift is occurring. I am getting to know myself. I like myself. Good, intentional self-care helps me heal. And to heal is to learn to live with the brokenness. Healing is moving forward, carrying my experiences with me.

It has taken two years for me to pick up a paint brush again. And then another year before I was willing to paint anything larger than the size of a piece of copy paper. Moving to a larger canvas has unleashed more feelings, more expression. Now, the paintings name themselves before they are painted. More images come forward from my sub-conscious:

The Wind Blows and the Flowers Dance is my metaphor for life. Walking along a road early one morning I saw dainty little white flowers effortlessly giving in to the wind. Life just is. As I began to lay out the painting, my hands cast distinct shadows on the canvas. Perfect. The hands became the shadows for the plants. Hands trying to grasp impermanence, wanting to control.

Red Wings. Charles is dead but still a powerful creative force as I express and feel the depth of his personality. He used to say, "I can tell how good a carpenter is by looking in his toolbox." I painted this as one of my tributes to him.

What Happened? I painted for me. I am that person who doesn't throw flowers away until they are a long time dead. Observing each stage from beginning bud to wrinkled, faded petals dropping—fascinating and beautiful. Like me, they are in transition and continue to express the cycle of life.

Ghost Tree symbolizes the impermanence of life, equanimity, and beauty. It continues to decay. It is a symbol of calm and composure as it invites in other life. And it is always beautiful, no matter what.

Are You There? This is one question that I ask as I look up at the night sky and remember Charles. It also contains my feeling of belonging.

Until now, emptiness and void were negatives. In art, vacant space is a place for the eye to rest. In life, emptiness is a ripe time. It is the beginning of increased self-awareness, full of all possibility, and creative potential.

39

Energy Continues

> "You did a good job. A good job of being a pleasure to know."
> *Lincoln in the Bardo* by George Saunders

A continuity of consciousness has survived Charles' death. There is an awareness of him that I can access anytime. At first, the loss of our earthly relationship is so great that I cannot see beyond it. Now that everything has fallen away, his spiritual presence remains.

When I need another opinion, I ask him. When I'm alone in a new situation, I tell him to be there for me. And, when I least expect it, his voice comes forward inside my head.

* * *

I can't quite reach the vase on the top shelf. Getting up my courage, I tell Norma who is holding the ladder, "If I go just one step higher, I'll be able to reach it."

An admonishing voice shouts in my head, "Don't you dare climb higher. You don't do well on ladders. Heights make you unsteady. Don't you dare."

"Norma, Charlie just told me not to climb any higher. I can't believe I just got his unsolicited opinion!"

It is amazing and wonderful to witness Charles' consciousness or energy continue. He still makes me smile. I feel free to talk about him and tell stories. And I appreciate when friends and family talk about him, too.

* * *

With Charlie's death I, too, know that I am so much more than my body. Albert Einstein declared, "Energy can neither be created nor destroyed; energy can only be transferred or changed from one form to another." Life and death and any space in between are different manifestations of energy.

My own equation which helps me is:

after death = after life = life after death.

Or, my own Living Bardo.

I notice that the extent to which I grasp this underlying concept, the more I relax as my life continues.

40

Creativity

"We are left with the impulse.
You reach for a glass that isn't there
and your hand swishes through empty air."
Advice for Future Corpses by Sallie Tisdale

I see now the importance and value of death. With loss, the cycle and the habits of my existence are broken. With death, the cycle of life is broken. There is complete disconnection with the past. I am immediately placed on a threshold of potential and possibility. An opportunity to discover myself and to reshape my life, if only I am able to have a slight shift in perspective and recognize it.

Under the stress of losing Charles, my memory defaulted to prior experiences and my behavior defaulted to prior practices. For a short time, the wounded child returned. Love, affirmation, encouragement, validation, and permission appeared to be outside of me beyond my control and reach. I was afraid and fell prey to the big, wide world of the unknown.

But it is when I let go of trying to control outcome and results, when I am most vulnerable and exposed, that I am able to discover the creative potential in my life. When I express my creativity, I am soothed. It also makes me realize the depth of my character, mind, soul, and faith. This depth helps me stand on solid ground again. If I can say who I am, then I can stand tall.

The desire to know myself, to know who I am is what drives me forward to paint in my studio. I meditate. I paint. I write. I persevere. Discipline supports my creativity. It is a regular practice that sets aside alone time. I quiet myself and listen for my inner voice to speak. I am guided. My creativity is expressed. I am present and deeply satisfied.

Many small disappointments simply disappear. With extreme loss a new baseline is created. I am able to see life's events more easily with detachment. As I observe myself, my thoughts and behavior, I see when I am hurt by taking situations too personally. Then, I can shift my perspective, adjust and either let go or seek to respond compassionately.

Transformation involves death and resurrection:

Life, death, resurrection.

Life, death, transformation.

Life, death, renewal.

These three constitute a much greater cycle that remains unbroken. Death is a big force. Life is a big force. These are beyond my control. But, my resurrection, renewal, and rebirth

I create by the choices I make. These choices are only limited by my ability to orient life towards a future of my own creation.

I am alive and while I am alive, I want to be fully alive. I want to be present, like a child, and not miss a thing. I want to wake up looking forward to the day and fall asleep feeling I gave it my best. I want to be open, aware, receptive.

I want to get out of my small world and be a person who is there for others. Death changes the meaning of 'sacrifice'. I sacrifice nothing by loving. As friends, we invest in each other, unafraid, because we have nothing to lose.

Life is a meditation, the practice of being present. The more I live with that awareness, the easier my life becomes.

41

Smiling Is a Choice

"Only to try is important."
Breakfast with Buddha by Roland Merullo

Every day I make myself leave the house to be around other people, even if we don't speak or interact. I go to the grocery; I run small errands. Over time I notice that I am talking to strangers more and more. Words just come out of my mouth. I might be standing next to someone who is also contemplating which salad to buy. "Have you tried these before?" I ask.

I am learning to help myself. Recognizing when I am down is a start. Sometimes I just choose to be down. Giving myself a simple routine helps. I get up about the same time every day, wash my face, brush my teeth, get dressed. Especially when I don't feel like it, I make an extra effort to look nice and put on a little makeup. It all helps. Everything is incremental. Working out at the gym is a life saver. I feel a little better afterwards, no matter what.

I am trying. I am practicing. When I am walking with my head down, I tell myself, heads up. Slowly I am becoming aware that smiling is a choice.

42

I Am Whole

"... the open heart, the happy exhaustion, something beyond you, which is people to play with. Play ... brings us into the now."
Almost Anything by Anne Lamott

For the last two years, it has been my turn to host Thanksgiving and this year I'm really going to do it. I'm always surprised when people say, "yes," to my invitations. Maybe it's because I have felt incomplete, like half of me is missing.

In my life, I entertain easily. I set the stage. Then it's up to everyone to have a good time. Once, a friend volunteered to vacuum. "Why bother," was my response. "This place will fill up with people and no one will be looking down."

What starts as eight guests grows to ten, then twelve, thirteen. And now, there will be fifteen, with two additional people stopping by for drinks. Everyone is enthusiastic, glad to see that I'm up for hosting. A milestone, for sure.

They also recognize I need help. We are all looking forward to the celebration. I orchestrate and no one refuses my requests.

Will you help me move the furniture? Could you do the centerpieces?

As host, the turkey and stuffing are my responsibility. Charlie always enjoyed roasting the bird, so it has been many years since I've roasted one. Looking on the internet, I settle on an overnight slow roast recipe and two recipes for dressing, baked separately.

On the big day tables are set, looking festive and inviting. Smiling, joyful friends arrive with appetizers, homemade bread, mashed potatoes, sweet potatoes, cranberry sauce, salad, green vegetables, and pies with whipped cream. And bottles of wine.

Thanks for opening the wine and seeing to it that people have drinks.

I appreciate you making a fire in the fireplace.

Together we decide when the turkey is done. It comes out to rest, looking like a proud tasty bird. Food that needs warming goes into the medium-hot oven.

I am so glad you are making the gravy.

Thank you for carving the bird.

Yes, I thought we would have a buffet. Go ahead and organize the food along this counter.

Finally, the magic moment arrives. We all gather around the tables, standing by our chairs. Each year we begin with a special toast, usually led by the host. I know that I cannot do it and have asked one of these dear friends to step in:

"We raise a glass to all of our family, friends, and loved ones who cannot be with us today."

Moving Forward

"Worshipping the dead is not the business of the living."
Antigone by Sophocles

I choose pink granite for the stone slab bench at the cemetery. My hope is that pink looks less dismal in rain and drizzle. Being at the end of the row next to a grassy easement, the bench is easy to spot. Overcast and dreary since my arrival, I have driven by several times, noticing but not stopping. It looks cold and lonely. I'll wait and go on a sunny day.

Each year for the last three, I have planted perennial flowers at either end of the bench. And like the other years, I come and see they did not survive. Probably deer, or lack of attention. I give up. Nothing will make this spot cozy or more inviting. What I do notice is the grass seed we raked into the bare soil has sprouted and is growing. The bench now looks like it has integrated into the 'community,' of graves.

I am here and I am not here.

know why I feel a special call this year to make ourney. I feel detached as I visit family and this very familiar loved village. Perhaps it is the missing. Perhaps I can see how I have moved on.

I feel pain, teary, and a pounding in my heart as I approach. I sit on this bench, Charlie's bench, and touch all the emotions and memories of the day we buried his ashes. I realize now how numb and in an altered state I was that day.

* * *

I take one long-stemmed pale white rose from the fifty roses in the bucket next to his grave and gently set it in the small square black hole in the ground. Others come forward to distribute the remaining roses.

"Granny? Can I do that?" quietly asks young Liam.

"Of course. Just be careful because there are thorns."

As if the grave were a vase, a bouquet of large fat roses appears to rise up out of the ground.

"Are we really going to do this?" asks my daughter. All eyes are fixed on this gorgeous growing bouquet.

"Yes," is my answer.

In silence, with fifty people looking on, I begin to shovel dirt into the hole, on top of the roses. Robert, my brother-in-law, takes the shovel from my hand and slowly continues. Then, his son, my nephew, Forrest.

Touching my arm to get my attention, Liam whispers, "Can I do that, too?"

I nod.

Liam approaches his adult cousin and lightly touches his bent over back. In slow motion, Forrest stops, turns, sees little Liam and looks at me. Again I nod, and he hands over the shovel.

Then comes Liam's father, Kieran, and a spontaneous ceremony of filling the grave and burying the roses begins. I have no idea how many join in. I watch as shovels full of dirt are tenderly, slowly, poured on top of the roses until there is a large mound of earth covering the grave.

I cannot stop staring at that mound of dirt. Oblivious to others, I climb on top and furiously start stomping. Robert joins me. Together we stomp and stamp, beating and releasing some of our hurt until the earth is flat.

* * *

Sitting here today, I realize life has moved me forward. I am more detached. I see a pendulum swinging. In this moment, I know I have recreated myself and probably will have to recreate myself several more times.

As I allow these thoughts and feelings to wash over me, why I am here becomes clear: I am here to remember, to honor, and to feel gratitude for our time together.

Thank you, Charles.

An Afterlife for My Living

"Hamlet (speaking to Rosencrantz about Denmark being a prison):
'Why then 'tis none to you, for there is nothing either good
or bad but thinking makes it so."
Hamlet by William Shakespeare

Shakespeare's words written over four-hundred years ago still resonate for me today. As I observe myself, everything originates in my mind. Depending on my mood my self-image changes. Moment by moment. How fragile and temporary my view of life is!

Grief mixed with fear created a terror that did not serve me. This mixture caused an unwinding of my self-confidence and self-esteem. I produced deteriorating chains of thoughts for myself, by myself, inside my head.

From: have I done enough (. . . enough work, enough prevention, enough self-care. . .) to, am I enough (maybe I should be better, work harder. . .), descending to, am I worthy? (Do I deserve to be happy? Have I earned it?). Resulting in:

Doubt. Panic. Anxiety. This suffering colored my world and created distress.

I need to be *en garde*. My body can no longer withstand the pain of grief, the pain of loss. I can be immobilized, until, I see that I am the creator of my confusion, my negativity. Only then can I detach and choose to dismiss these demons as untrue, and create new positive energy for myself.

Wanting to move away from grief, I must believe in my ability to heal. Creating new 'mantras', I say over and over again in my head: I deserve a high quality of life. I make good choices. I am supported. I am not alone.

Emotions are part of my innate energy and part of my passion. They can change quickly which empowers me. I can feed an emotion or choose another. Or, I can observe it, not act and then notice the effect that it has on me.

As I experience the range of my emotions, I begin to witness multiple concurrent feelings. A friend shares some good news. I see how happy she is. I am sincerely happy for her and share her moment. Outside of the sadness that I continually feel, I can feel happy for her at the same time.

I go to a movie and it envelops me. I start with surprise and shock as the murder mystery unfolds. I share the lead actor's emotions of fear and passion. Maybe I have temporarily left my life, but the feelings which I brought with me into the theatre are still accessible. I cry along with the characters. I am experiencing the thrill of the movie while experiencing my sadness at the same time.

How do I heal? I embrace my loss fully. I carry it as a part of me always. And I continue to experience my life as it is today. This is what it feels like to be alone in my house, claim it, and rearrange the furniture as I like it. This is how I dress without consideration for anyone else. This is how I create and feel satisfaction and success. I own my feelings. I write them; I paint them.

My life has been a Living Bardo, full of transitions. Many endings and beginnings, all interwoven, intertwined, and overlapped. Poignant and ecstatic like veins in marble creating beauty, I have seen how sadness tempers happiness—giving it more depth, making it sweeter. I wept at my grandson's fifth grade graduation as I smiled with pride and love.

I like the feeling of containment. Not containment meaning restriction, but an openness that is walled by trust, trust in the Divine. The Divine in me is the love I continue to feel. The more I trust, the more I have faith, the more I can drop the illusion of control and allow life to unfold, to come to me.

Openness is a special kind of emptiness. It is an invitation to bring on the possibilities, the choices. Openness doesn't ignore life's experiences, it brings them along in the form of presence, clarity, and compassion. Openness creates freedom and awareness. And it implies independence.

Today, Charlie is in my heart. And I am free—free to laugh, to grow, to move forward.

Part Four

The Poems

Are You There?
Terre Reed
February, 2019
30" X 36"
Oil on Canvas

To view this painting in color, go to
TerreReed.com

I Am Ungrounded
by Terre Reed

My house is neutral,
But my emotions dash about
Daring me to take control.
Why this chaos?
Why this conflict?
Fighting sleep,
Fighting age, fighting aloneness,
Sometimes fighting the smile.

Acceptance

by Terre Reed

Dreaming, walls crush me.
I brace myself and compel life.
Struggle is my resistance.

I cannot take death on.
I can only wake up
And live today.

My Gates

by Terre Reed

Each time I write, I slide
Deeper into my own feelings.
I am becoming more intimate
With myself.

And when I paint, I am
Stimulated but calm, alert and
Alive to my world. I create my
Satisfaction.

From seeds planted, fragile
Miracles emerge with two leaves.
Beyond understanding, I can only
Nurture.

Grateful for the gifts, beauty
Rises out of grief. I release resistance
And denial. My heart softened, I accept
Life.

Life's Juice
by Terre Reed

Laughing at uncertainty,
Unafraid of possibilities,
I stand on worthiness and faith.

Taking what is mine,
Owning this moment,
The joy, the depth, the value of love.

Life comes uninhibited.
Grateful, I choose now.
The past, the present, coexist.

Choice
by Terre Reed

Abandon, embrace.

Do not underestimate the effect
You have on other People.

Do not underestimate the effect
You have on yourself.

Yes to It All

by Terre Reed

Yes to work,
Choices,
Passion.

Yes to focus,
Perseverance,
Satisfaction.

Yes to duality,
Change,
Surprise.

Yes to myself,
Beautiful,
Acccpting.

My Prayer

by Terre Reed

Distinct individuals,
With faith in experience,
Values, tender heart dualities,
Color, texture, surprise, and growth.

Life's impulse opens,
Participating and creating,
Aware of treasure, in gratitude
We go forward, a gift to each other.

Love Comes to My Aid

by Terre Reed

Quiet Sunday morning streets hold mystery,
Memories of last night, of yesterday,
Of all the time that has passed
Since your departure.

Remembering your presence, feeling the absence.
You will always be my Dear Sweet Charles.
My heart is moved and
My eyes are moist.

With tenderness, I observe, store, and proceed.
Spirit gently expanding my awareness.
So much I do not understand.
Yet, I go forward.

Broadcasting Spring with sweet harmony,
Birds celebrate new life, creation.
No longer crying with loss,
I accept their speak.

The pendulum swings between pain and joy.
Seamless, never one without the other,
Humorous in the worst moments,
Pain enriching joy easing pain.

Looking for My Life
by Terre Reed

Lost, broken, scattered,
I am hammered.
I am reshaped.

Life is now wide open,
Past experience,
A baseline.

I carry with me
A tenderness
No longer buried.

Happiness is now
Celebration
No longer betrayal.

A sweetness propels me,
Wrapping pain.
I have been loved.
I am loved.
I love.

Epilogue

Three Years Have Passed

"Family love is the best practice for dying.
For understanding you are part of something big.
Not just one body."
Breakfast with Buddha by Roland Merullo

"Granny?" asks the backseat.

"Liam," I acknowledge.

"I can get us home from here." Liam is eleven now. It's the last night of my visit. We're on our way home from dinner and ice cream. "See that sign over there? That's where I go for triathlon practice. I'm sure I know the way."

"OK, Liam. You're the navigator. Take us home."

"Just stay on this road. Keep going. I'll tell you when to turn. We're not there yet."

"Are we close? Make sure you give me enough time to turn on the turn signal."

"I will. Just keep going. We're not there yet."

"You know, Liam. It won't be too many more visits before you will be driving me!"

"Excuse me, Granny, but do you think you'll live that long?"

"Just how old do you think you have to be to drive?" the smiling front seat asks.

"I don't know, twenty?"

"No, I think it is before then. I don't know the age in this state. You would have to ask your dad. But I'm guessing maybe sixteen or seventeen."

"Really?" Pause. "In five years?" Pause again. "Granny? I think you'll make it."

"Well, you certainly know what death is."

"Un huh."

"How much further?" I ask, continuing to drive home. "Nothing is familiar."

"Just keep going," he says, "I'll tell you when. I am looking for the big blue sign. There it is. See it, Granny? It says 'Chase'. We turn just after that sign."

"Good job, Liam." I recognize the neighborhood. We are almost home.

School tomorrow. Time to shower, brush teeth, and go to bed.

"OK Granny. I'm ready," Liam calls from his room. I go in to give him a kiss and say good night.

"I won't be here when you wake up in the morning," I tell him. "I'm leaving on a very early flight. So, this is good night until I see you in a couple of months." He pops up onto his knees to give me a very special hug.

"Liam, Charlie has been gone quite a while now. And, I have to say, I think he is my angel. He looks out for me. It's just something I know inside. It's not that he has a shape. It's more of a feeling."

"Maybe, Charlie could be my angel, too?"

"Certainly."

"Good night. Granny, I love you."

"Good night, Liam. Sleep well. I love you, too."

Vocabulary of the Living Bardo

I share the following schematic with you as a part of my thought process and evolution.

Sorting out my feelings, I realize vocabulary around grief evolves into its own time line. This vocabulary is done in a stream-of-consciousness manner. As a word comes into my head, I write it down.

It soon became evident that the words fell into three significant categories: Loss, Transition, and Renewal. Some words reoccurred. I figured they must be significant, so I wrote these in all caps. I found this exercise very thought provoking, reflective, and healing.

Perhaps you will identify with where you are on your journey. Perhaps you will add more words.

Vocabulary of Loss

DEATH, BELONGING, abandonment, isolation, habit, LOVE,

shattered, diminished, order, fragmented, fear, QUESTIONS,

UNCOMFORATABLE, unimportant, defense, pain, past,

worthless, static, flat, OPPOSITES, UNCERTAINTY, hopeless,

closed, protection, SURRENDER, memories, stillness,

nothing, EMOTIONS, CONTROL, GOALS, absence,

complicated, deeper, DEPRESSION, expectations, emptiness,

ending, myself, RELATIONSHIP, disappointment, shame,

chaotic, escape, structure, TOMORROW, FANTASY,

FLOATING, ANXIETY, CONTINUITY, final, disbelief,

heaviness, suffering, goodbye, magnitude, empty, decay,

loneliness, grief, containment, VULNERABLE, CONFUSION,

sadness, WOUNDEDNESS, nausea, missing, BROKEN,

GRASPING, primal, invisible, longing, FAMILY, sorrow, panic,

unprotected, separation, CONNECTION, ambiguity, raw, fight,

impact, CONTEMPLATION, CONTROL, MEANING, struggle,

frail, fatigue, isolation, FAITH, PRECIOUS, reacting,

unbalanced, ANTICIPATION, denial, perfection, exhaustion,

pushing

Vocabulary of Transition

LOVE, CONTEMPATION, ANXIETY, distraction, observer, overwhelming, understanding, MEANING, CONFUSION, CURISOTY, journey, discover, MEDITATION, ANTICIPATION, tenderness, SAFETY, FAITH, neediness, INTENTION, hunger, HEART, MINDFUL, UNCOMFORTABLE, underground, trust, WOUNDEDNESS, CREATIVITY, CONTROL, UNDERTAINITY, MYSTERY, inertia, QUESTIONS, process, LIFE, VALUE, HEALING, OPEN, movement, COMMUNITY, exploring, duality, knowledge, tolerance, willingness, patterns, problems, solutions, shutdown, delusions, possibilities,

ALONE, hiding, FLOATING, coexistence, impermanence, SILENCE, COMPASSION, survival, CYCLE, asking, SURRENDER, spirituality, VULNERABLE, BEGINNING, SHIFT, path, perspective, failure, simple, acknowledge, BROKEN, GUIDANCE, details, LISTENING, evolving, self-awareness, UNFOLDING, choices, continuum, ENERGY, inner-state, outer-state, arc, incorporation, ALLOW, relief, FANTASY, touch, fulcrum, release, GRASPING, COMPANIONSHIP, synthesis, FLOW, DEPRESSION, comfort, affection, reaching, CONSCIOUSNESS, JOY, ACCEPTANCE, VALIDATION, gentleness, RHYTHM, COURAGE, FAMILY, discipline, learning, search

Vocabulary of Renewal

LOVE, MINDFUL, growing, UNFOLDING, INTENTION, BALANCE, NEWNESS, BEGINNING, ALLOW, passion, SAFETY, rebirth, laughter, focus, awe, fearless, celebration, BELONGING, relaxing, MYSTERY, MEDITATION, timing, embrace, COMPANSIONSHIP, gifts, HEALING, CREATIVITY, RHYTHM, patience, VALUE, LIFE, answers, generosity, UNCERTAINITY, COMMUNITY, HEART, reclaim, authenticity, FUTURE, wholeness, ALONE, COMPASSION, PRECIOUS, desire, wisdom, SILENCE, RELATIONSHIP, self-esteem, alive, CONSCIOUSNESS, SURRENDER, art, intimacy, play, unknown, path, poetry, EMOTIONS, OPEN, FLOW, action, growth, CYCLE, QUESTIONS, music, JOY, writing awake, CURIOSITY, choice, GOALS, LISTENING, present, flexibility, purpose, emergence, GUIDANCE, peace, knowing, contribution. self-compassion, FAMILY, TOMORROW, calm, empathy, CONNECTION, ACCEPTANCE, ENERGY, satisfaction, COURAGE, CONTEMPLATION, colorful, becoming, individual, alignment, spirit, DEATH, share, power, grace

Bibliography

Albom, Mitch. *Tuesdays with Morrie.* New York: Broadway Books, 1997, 2017.

Brown, Brene. *The Gifts of Imperfection.* Center City: Hazelden, 2010.

Campbell, Joseph. *Hero with a Thousand Faces.* NPR Interview, by Bill Moyer, 1988.

Chodron, Pema. *Comfortable with Uncertainty.* Boulder: Shambhala, 2018.

Dideon, Joan. *The Year of Magical Thinking.* New York: Alfred Knopf, Vintage Books, 2005.

Kay, Buddy. Wisc, Frcd. Lyrics "A' You're Adorable." Lippman, Sid. Music. RCA Victor, 1948.

Lama, HH Dalai. *The Tibetan Book of the Dead, Introduction.* New York: Penquin Books, 2006.

LaMott, Anne. *Almost Anything*. New York: Riverhead Books imprint of Random House, 2018.

Lewis, C.S. *A Grief Observed*. New York: HarperCollins, 2009.

Merullo, Roland. *Breakfast with Buddha*. Chapel Hill: Algonquin Books, 2017.

Ortega y Gasset, Jose. *Some Lessons in Metaphysics*. Toronto and New York. George J. McLeod Limited, 1966, 1969.

Sterling, Andrew B., King, Robert. "Bridget O'Flynn (Where've Ya Been?)." Victor Talking Machine Company, 1926.

Prechtel, Martin. *The Smell of Rain on Dust*. Berkeley: North Atlantic Books, 2015.

Rinpoche, Pema. "The Four Essential Points of Letting Go." *The Lion's Roar Newsletter* (7/15/2017).

Roberts, Barbara K. *Death without Denial, Grief without Apology*. Troutdale: New Sage Press, 2002.

Shakespeare, William. *Romeo and Juliet*. 1597-1623.

Saunders, George. *Lincoln in the Bardo*. New York: Penguin Random House, 2019.

Sophocles. *Antigone*. 441 BC.

Tisdale, Sallie. *Advice for Future Corpses*. New York: Touchstone, 2018.

Tuwaletstiwa, Judy. *Retrospective Exhibition*. Perf. Judy Tuwaletstiwa, Santa Fe, New Mexico 2019. Document.

Weidman, Paul. "Mirror Images and Meaning in Ancestral Pueblo Pottery." *Pasatiempo, Santa Fe New Mexican,* 2019.

Whitson, Beath Slater. Lyrics "Let Me Call You Sweetheart." Friedman, Leo. Music. Columbia Records, 1910.

Acknowledgments

As I sat with the idea of this book, I realized I felt called to write it. For four years, every time I was ready for the next step, an appropriate door opened. People appeared who gave me advice, guidance, and professional help.

Thank you to Lydia Clark, Wayne Mueller, Michael Harkavy and Kathryn Stedham. You made significant contributions to my personal growth and the quality of the book. Thank you also to Rhee Sheck for her initial editing and observations. And thank you to Joy Cunningham and Ana and Sergio Palacios Perez for their moral support and friendship.

All of the photography in the book was done by Leland D. Shaeffer. Thank you.

And special thanks to all of my family and friends who shored me up during my healing, especially my daughter Jennifer and her husband Kieran. And of course, Liam.

Meet the Author

Terre Reed

Terre Reed is fearless in her willingness to express emotion and allow the reader into the intimate experience of loss, death, and healing. An observer of the obvious, her zany sense of humor will make you laugh in the middle of her pain.

A diverse, high energy person, Terre continues to live in Santa Fe, New Mexico, home for over forty years. She brings passion and intensity to both work and play. As an artist, she mixes her own colors to capture just the right tone, mood, and nuance. As a master gardener she announces, "I am growing a state fair award-winning pumpkin this year. And since the fair has been canceled, I'll be the judge."

Her impetus for this book was her husband's sudden illness and subsequent death. A series of emails to update family and friends became bedrock material. Her experience and processing of profound loss and personal transition culminate in this book of vivid paintings, soulful poetry, and deeply personal ruminations on life.

We all benefit as Terre shares her journey. She gives the reader permission to revisit, to retell their story, and to heal.

TerreReed.com

CPSIA information can be obtained
at www.ICGtesting.com
Printed in the USA
FSHW022122211020
74895FS